C Is for Calm: A Calming Journal for Kids

Yvelette Stines

C Is for Calm: A Calming Journal for Kids

Copyright 2020 by Yvelette Stines
ISBN: 978-0-9849990-5-7

Gratitude

With humility I thank God, my family, friends, supporters, community, and ancestors.

Yves Stines, Bettye Stines, Bettina Ortez, Joshua Ortez, Kinyel Friday, Niki Johnson, Victoria C. Rowan Julie D. Andrews, Dr. Linda Nabha-Selim, Dr. LeConte Dill, Dr. Elaine Carey, Gwen Jimmere, Elizabeth Whittaker-Walker, Charlena Ponders, Francina James, Rebecca Rudnicki, Louise Spector, and Ashlee Chesny.

Introduction

C Is for Calm: A Calming Journal for Kids is a journal that has writing prompts and affirmations that will help children understand their feelings, thoughts, and find their inner calm.

Young scholars will enjoy writing, drawing, and coloring. The book has 21 entries. It serves as an introduction to journaling. Enjoy the journal, affirmations, and living a calm and peaceful life.

C Is for Calm: A Calming Journal for Kids

Belongs To:

Date: S M T W TH F S __ / __ / ____

☺ Today I Feel ☹

Happy	Silly	Excited	Loved	Scared
Sad	Mad	Disappointed	Lonely	Safe

I Feel This Way Because

1. _____

2. _____

3. _____

Draw or write about a time you felt calm.

Did anyone or anything make you feel happy today?

Did anyone or anything make you feel sad today?

Did anyone or anything make you laugh today?

Did anyone or anything make you cry today?

Did anyone or anything make you feel loved today?

Did anyone or anything make you feel lonely today?

Did anyone or anything make you feel safe today?

Did anyone or anything make you feel scared today?

Write or draw about the most favorite part of your day.

 Write or draw about the least favorite part of your day.

Date: S M T W TH F S __ /__ /____

☺ Today I Feel ☹

Happy   Silly   Excited   Loved   Scared

Sad   Mad   Disappointed   Lonely   Safe

I Feel This Way Because

1. _____

2. _____

3. _____

Draw or write about a time you felt calm.

Did anyone or anything make you feel happy today?

Did anyone or anything make you feel sad today?

Did anyone or anything make you laugh today?

Did anyone or anything make you cry today?

Did anyone or anything make you feel loved today?

Did anyone or anything make you feel lonely today?

Did anyone or anything make you feel safe today?

Did anyone or anything make you feel scared today?

Write or draw about the most favorite part of your day.

 Write or draw about the least favorite part of your day.

Date: S M T W TH F S __ / __ / ____

☺ Today I Feel ☹

Happy	Silly	Excited	Loved	Scared
Sad	Mad	Disappointed	Lonely	Safe

I Feel This Way Because

1. _____

2. _____

3. _____

Draw or write about a time you felt calm.

Did anyone or anything make you feel happy today?

Did anyone or anything make you feel sad today?

Did anyone or anything make you laugh today?

Did anyone or anything make you cry today?

Did anyone or anything make you feel loved today?

Did anyone or anything make you feel lonely today?

Did anyone or anything make you feel safe today?

Did anyone or anything make you feel scared today?

Write or draw about the most favorite part of your day.

 Write or draw about the least favorite part of your day.

Date: S M T W TH F S __ / __ / ____

☺ Today I Feel ☹

Happy	Silly	Excited	Loved	Scared
Sad	Mad	Disappointed	Lonely	Safe

I Feel This Way Because

1. _____

2. _____

3. _____

Draw or write about a time you felt calm.

Did anyone or anything make you feel happy today?

Did anyone or anything make you feel sad today?

Did anyone or anything make you laugh today?

Did anyone or anything make you cry today?

Did anyone or anything make you feel loved today?

Did anyone or anything make you feel lonely today?

Did anyone or anything make you feel safe today?

Did anyone or anything make you feel scared today?

Write or draw about the most favorite part of your day.

 Write or draw about the least favorite part of your day.

Date: S M T W TH F S __ /__ /____

☺ Today I Feel ☹

Happy	Silly	Excited	Loved	Scared
Sad	Mad	Disappointed	Lonely	Safe

I Feel This Way Because

1. _____

2. _____

3. _____

Draw or write about a time you felt calm.

Did anyone or anything make you feel happy today?

Did anyone or anything make you feel sad today?

Did anyone or anything make you laugh today?

Did anyone or anything make you cry today?

Did anyone or anything make you feel loved today?

Did anyone or anything make you feel lonely today?

Did anyone or anything make you feel safe today?

Did anyone or anything make you feel scared today?

Write or draw about the most favorite part of your day.

 Write or draw about the least favorite part of your day.

Date: S M T W TH F S __ / __ / ____

☺ Today I Feel ☹

Happy	Silly	Excited	Loved	Scared
Sad	Mad	Disappointed	Lonely	Safe

I Feel This Way Because

1. _____

2. _____

3. _____

Draw or write about a time you felt calm.

Did anyone or anything make you feel happy today?

Did anyone or anything make you feel sad today?

Did anyone or anything make you laugh today?

Did anyone or anything make you cry today?

Did anyone or anything make you feel loved today?

Did anyone or anything make you feel lonely today?

Did anyone or anything make you feel safe today?

Did anyone or anything make you feel scared today?

Write or draw about the most favorite part of your day.

 Write or draw about the least favorite part of your day.

Date: S M T W TH F S __ / __ / ____

☺ Today I Feel ☹

Happy	Silly	Excited	Loved	Scared
Sad	Mad	Disappointed	Lonely	Safe

I Feel This Way Because

1. _____

2. _____

3. _____

Draw or write about a time you felt calm.

Did anyone or anything make you feel happy today?

Did anyone or anything make you feel sad today?

Did anyone or anything make you laugh today?

Did anyone or anything make you cry today?

Did anyone or anything make you feel loved today?

Did anyone or anything make you feel lonely today?

Did anyone or anything make you feel safe today?

Did anyone or anything make you feel scared today?

Write or draw about the most favorite part of your day.

 Write or draw about the least favorite part of your day.

Date: S M T W TH F S __ / __ / ____

☺ Today I Feel ☹

Happy	Silly	Excited	Loved	Scared
Sad	Mad	Disappointed	Lonely	Safe

I Feel This Way Because

1. _____

2. _____

3. _____

Draw or write about a time you felt calm.

Did anyone or anything make you feel happy today?

Did anyone or anything make you feel sad today?

Did anyone or anything make you laugh today?

Did anyone or anything make you cry today?

Did anyone or anything make you feel loved today?

Did anyone or anything make you feel lonely today?

Did anyone or anything make you feel safe today?

Did anyone or anything make you feel scared today?

Write or draw about the most favorite part of your day.

 Write or draw about the least favorite part of your day.

Date: S M T W TH F S __ / __ / ____

☺ Today I Feel ☹

Happy	Silly	Excited	Loved	Scared
Sad	Mad	Disappointed	Lonely	Safe

I Feel This Way Because

1. _____

2. _____

3. _____

Draw or write about a time you felt calm.

Did anyone or anything make you feel happy today?

Did anyone or anything make you feel sad today?

Did anyone or anything make you laugh today?

Did anyone or anything make you cry today?

Did anyone or anything make you feel loved today?

Did anyone or anything make you feel lonely today?

Did anyone or anything make you feel safe today?

Did anyone or anything make you feel scared today?

Write or draw about the most favorite part of your day.

 Write or draw about the least favorite part of your day.

Date: S M T W TH F S __ /__ /____

☺ Today I Feel ☹

Happy   Silly   Excited   Loved   Scared

Sad   Mad   Disappointed Lonely   Safe

I Feel This Way Because

1. _____

2. _____

3. _____

Draw or write about a time you felt calm.

Did anyone or anything make you feel happy today?

Did anyone or anything make you feel sad today?

Did anyone or anything make you laugh today?

Did anyone or anything make you cry today?

Did anyone or anything make you feel loved today?

Did anyone or anything make you feel lonely today?

Did anyone or anything make you feel safe today?

Did anyone or anything make you feel scared today?

Write or draw about the most
favorite part of your day.

 Write or draw about the least
favorite part of your day.

Date: S M T W TH F S __ / __ / ____

☺ Today I Feel ☹

Happy	Silly	Excited	Loved	Scared
Sad	Mad	Disappointed	Lonely	Safe

I Feel This Way Because

1. _____

2. _____

3. _____

Draw or write about a time you felt calm.

Did anyone or anything make you feel happy today?

Did anyone or anything make you feel sad today?

Did anyone or anything make you laugh today?

Did anyone or anything make you cry today?

Did anyone or anything make you feel loved today?

Did anyone or anything make you feel lonely today?

Did anyone or anything make you feel safe today?

Did anyone or anything make you feel scared today?

Write or draw about the most favorite part of your day.

 Write or draw about the least favorite part of your day.

Date: S M T W TH F S __ / __ / ____

☺ Today I Feel ☹

Happy	Silly	Excited	Loved	Scared
Sad	Mad	Disappointed	Lonely	Safe

I Feel This Way Because

1. _____

2. _____

3. _____

Draw or write about a time you felt calm.

Did anyone or anything make you feel happy today?

Did anyone or anything make you feel sad today?

Did anyone or anything make you laugh today?

Did anyone or anything make you cry today?

Did anyone or anything make you feel loved today?

Did anyone or anything make you feel lonely today?

Did anyone or anything make you feel safe today?

Did anyone or anything make you feel scared today?

Write or draw about the most favorite part of your day.

 Write or draw about the least favorite part of your day.

Date: S M T W TH F S __ / __ / ____

☺ Today I Feel ☹

Happy	Silly	Excited	Loved	Scared
Sad	Mad	Disappointed	Lonely	Safe

I Feel This Way Because

1. _____

2. _____

3. _____

Draw or write about a time you felt calm.

Did anyone or anything make you feel happy today?

Did anyone or anything make you feel sad today?

Did anyone or anything make you laugh today?

Did anyone or anything make you cry today?

Did anyone or anything make you feel loved today?

Did anyone or anything make you feel lonely today?

Did anyone or anything make you feel safe today?

Did anyone or anything make you feel scared today?

Write or draw about the most favorite part of your day.

 Write or draw about the least favorite part of your day.

Date: S M T W TH F S __ / __ / ____

☺ Today I Feel ☹

Happy   Silly   Excited   Loved   Scared

Sad   Mad   Disappointed   Lonely   Safe

I Feel This Way Because

1. _____

2. _____

3. _____

Draw or write about a time you felt calm.

Did anyone or anything make you feel happy today?

Did anyone or anything make you feel sad today?

Did anyone or anything make you laugh today?

Did anyone or anything make you cry today?

Did anyone or anything make you feel loved today?

Did anyone or anything make you feel lonely today?

Did anyone or anything make you feel safe today?

Did anyone or anything make you feel scared today?

Write or draw about the most favorite part of your day.

 Write or draw about the least favorite part of your day.

Date: S M T W TH F S __ / __ / ____

☺ Today I Feel ☹

Happy	Silly	Excited	Loved	Scared
Sad	Mad	Disappointed	Lonely	Safe

I Feel This Way Because

1. _____

2. _____

3. _____

Draw or write about a time you felt calm.

Did anyone or anything make you feel happy today?

Did anyone or anything make you feel sad today?

Did anyone or anything make you laugh today?

Did anyone or anything make you cry today?

Did anyone or anything make you feel loved today?

Did anyone or anything make you lonely today?

Did anyone or anything make you feel safe today?

Did anyone or anything make you feel scared today?

Write or draw about the most favorite part of your day.

 Write or draw about the least favorite part of your day.

Date: S M T W TH F S __ /__ /____

☺ Today I Feel ☹

Happy   Silly   Excited   Loved   Scared

Sad   Mad   Disappointed   Lonely   Safe

I Feel This Way Because

1. _____

2. _____

3. _____

Draw or write about a time you felt calm.

Did anyone or anything make you feel happy today?

Did anyone or anything make you feel sad today?

Did anyone or anything make you laugh today?

Did anyone or anything make you cry today?

Did anyone or anything make you feel loved today?

Did anyone or anything make you feel lonely today?

Did anyone or anything make you feel safe today?

Did anyone or anything make you feel scared today?

Write or draw about the most favorite part of your day.

 Write or draw about the least favorite part of your day.

Date: S M T W TH F S __ /__ /____

☺ **Today I Feel** ☹

Happy	Silly	Excited	Loved	Scared
Sad	Mad	Disappointed	Lonely	Safe

I Feel This Way Because

1. _____

2. _____

3. _____

Draw or write about a time you felt calm.

Did anyone or anything make you feel happy today?

Did anyone or anything make you feel sad today?

Did anyone or anything make you laugh today?

Did anyone or anything make you cry today?

Did anyone or anything make you feel loved today?

Did anyone or anything make you feel lonely today?

Did anyone or anything make you feel safe today?

Did anyone or anything make you feel scared today?

Write or draw about the most favorite part of your day.

 Write or draw about the least favorite part of your day.

Date: S M T W TH F S __ / __ / ____

☺ Today I Feel ☹

Happy	Silly	Excited	Loved	Scared
Sad	Mad	Disappointed	Lonely	Safe

I Feel This Way Because

1. _____

2. _____

3. _____

Draw or write about a time you felt calm.

Did anyone or anything make you feel happy today?

Did anyone or anything make you feel sad today?

Did anyone or anything make you laugh today?

Did anyone or anything make you cry today?

Did anyone or anything make you feel loved today?

Did anyone or anything make you feel lonely today?

Did anyone or anything make you feel safe today?

Did anyone or anything make you feel scared today?

Write or draw about the most favorite part of your day.

 Write or draw about the least favorite part of your day.

Date: S M T W TH F S __ /__ /____

☺ Today I Feel ☹

Happy	Silly	Excited	Loved	Scared
Sad	Mad	Disappointed	Lonely	Safe

I Feel This Way Because

1. _____

2. _____

3. _____

Draw or write about a time you felt calm.

Did anyone or anything make you feel happy today?

Did anyone or anything make you feel sad today?

Did anyone or anything make you laugh today?

Did anyone or anything make you cry today?

Did anyone or anything make you feel loved today?

Did anyone or anything make you feel lonely today?

Did anyone or anything make you feel safe today?

Did anyone or anything make you feel scared today?

Write or draw about the most favorite part of your day.

 Write or draw about the least favorite part of your day.

Date: S M T W TH F S __ / __ / ___

☺ Today I Feel ☹

Happy   Silly   Excited   Loved   Scared

Sad   Mad   Disappointed   Lonely   Safe

I Feel This Way Because

1. _____

2. _____

3. _____

Draw or write about a time you felt calm.

Did anyone or anything make you feel happy today?

Did anyone or anything make you feel sad today?

Did anyone or anything make you laugh today?

Did anyone or anything make you cry today?

Did anyone or anything make you feel loved today?

Did anyone or anything make you feel lonely today?

Did anyone or anything make you feel safe today?

Did anyone or anything make you feel scared today?

Write or draw about the most favorite part of your day.

 Write or draw about the least favorite part of your day.

Date: S M T W TH F S __ / __ / ____

☺ Today I Feel ☹

Happy	Silly	Excited	Loved	Scared
Sad	Mad	Disappointed	Lonely	Safe

I Feel This Way Because

1. _____

2. _____

3. _____

Draw or write about a time you felt calm.

Did anyone or anything make you feel happy today?

Did anyone or anything make you feel sad today?

Did anyone or anything make you laugh today?

Did anyone or anything make you cry today?

Did anyone or anything make you feel loved today?

Did anyone or anything make you feel lonely today?

Did anyone or anything make you feel safe today?

Did anyone or anything make you feel scared today?

Write or draw about the most favorite part of your day.

 Write or draw about the least favorite part of your day.

Affirmations

Be Calm

C = Calm   I Am Calm

A = Able   I Am Able

L = Loving   I Am Loving

M = Mindful   I Am Mindful

Write and repeat the affirmation.

I Am Calm

1. _____

2. _____

3. _____

4. _____

Write or draw about a time you felt calm.

Write and repeat the affirmation.

I Am Able

1. _____

2. _____

3. _____

4. _____

Write or draw about a time you felt able.

Write and repeat the affirmation.

I Am Loving

1. _____

2. _____

3. _____

4. _____

Write or draw about a time you felt loving.

Write and repeat the affirmation.

I Am Mindful

1. _____

2. _____

3. _____

4. _____

Write or draw about a time you felt mindful.

I

Am

Calm

I

Am

Able

I

Am

Loving

I

Am

Mindful

About the Author

Yvelette Stines is a writer and educator. Her work has been published in Essence, Black Enterprise, Heart and Soul, The Root, The Source, Mind Body + Green, Purely Delicious Raw, GreenBuild + Design and more.

She coaches and teaches workshops to both children and adults on writing and wellness. Stines has a B.A. in Communication Studies, an M.Ed in Education, and M.S. Holistic Nutrition.

To learn more visit www.yvelettestines.com.

Made in the USA
Columbia, SC
15 May 2021